FOSSIL FUELS

This new edition published in 2005 by Smart Apple Media

2140 Howard Drive West, North Mankato, MN 56003

ISBN 1-58340-650-6

Design and production by EvansDay Design

Photographs: Frank Balthis, Gary Benson, Richard
Cummins, Image Finders (Michael Evans), Richard
Jacobs, Tom Myers, Unicorn Stock Photos (Eric
Berndt, Jean Higgin, Joe Sohm), NASA/Kennedy
Space Center

The Library of Congress has cataloged the earlier edition
as follows:

LIBRARY OF CONGRESS CATALOGING-IN-PUBLICATION DATA

Gibson, Diane, 1966–

Fossil fuels / by Diane Gibson.

p. cm. — (Sources of energy)

Includes index.

Summary: Introduces fossil fuels, describing where
and how they are found, refined, and used for energy.
Includes one simple experiment.

ISBN 1-887068-75-9

1. Fossil fuels—Juvenile literature. [1. Fossil fuels.

2. Power resources.] I. Title. II. Series.

TP318.3.G53   2000

553.2—dc21   99-055891

First paperback edition

9 8 7 6 5 4 3 2 1

fossilfuels

DIANE GIBSON

fossilfuels

Using a giant drill, workers dig into the earth.
Down the drill goes, burrowing through
hundreds of feet of dirt and rock. Suddenly,
the end of the drill breaks through a layer
of hard rock, and oil rushes up the hole and
shoots high into the air. Oil is a type of fossil fuel. So are coal and natural gas. Fossil
fuels are one of the most widely used
sources of energy in the world today.

⊙ FOSSIL FUELS WERE formed by prehistoric plants and animals. After these plants and animals died, layers of sand, clay, and dirt covered their remains. The remains were packed down tight, and the energy in them was stored up for millions of years. ◎ Some of the plants and animals turned to stone. These remains are called fossils. Many of the rest changed into coal, oil, and natural gas. Coal is a black or brown rock-like material. Oil is a liquid that can be dark green or black. Natural gas can be a **vapor** or a liquid.

SOME PREHISTORIC ANIMALS TURNED INTO FOSSILS; OTHERS BECAME FOSSIL FUELS.

FOSSIL FUELS ARE MADE
FROM THE ENERGY OF
PLANTS OF LONG AGO.

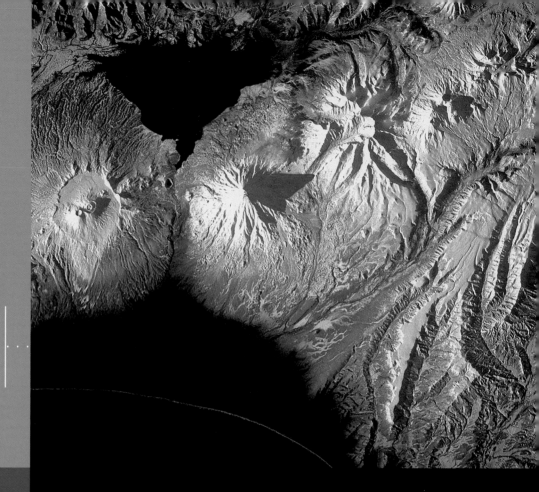

PHOTOGRAPHS TAKEN FROM HIGH ABOVE THE EARTH'S SURFACE CAN HELP GEOLOGISTS LOCATE BEDS OF COAL.

About 80 percent of homes throughout the world use fossil fuels for energy. Natural gas has no smell. Once the gas is brought up from the ground, an odor is added so that people can smell it. This makes it safer to use.

FINDING FOSSIL FUELS

⊙ LOCATING FOSSIL FUELS can take a lot of work. Geologists are scientists who study the earth's rocks and soil. By studying the way rocks are formed, geologists can tell if coal is under them. Sometimes, geologists also search for coal by studying photos taken by satellites as they circle the earth. ◈ Oil and natural gas are usually harder to find since they are found under many different types of rock. Often, sound is used to make a map of the ground. To do this, sound waves are sent into the ground. As they bounce back up, geologists can form an image of what lies underground. This is called seismic exploration. However, the only sure way to tell if oil and gas are under the ground is to drill into it. ◈ The country with the largest supply of coal is China—it produces nearly half of all the earth's coal. The Persian Gulf area produces more than one-fourth of the oil used in the world. Natural gas is found all over the world. The largest known **gas fields** are in Siberia and Texas.

PIPELINES ARE USED TO
CARRY GAS AND OIL TO RE-
FINERIES, WHERE THE FUEL
IS PREPARED FOR USE.

Coal is found in every continent around the world. One oil pipeline in North America is 1,771 miles (2,851 km) long, and a gas pipeline in Russia is 3,700 miles (5,957 km) long.

THE MOST EFFICIENT WAY TO TRANSPORT LARGE AMOUNTS OF COAL OVER LONG DISTANCES IS BY TRAIN.

MINING AND DRILLING

◉ COAL IS FOUND deep in the earth in strips called seams. Workers use big machines to dig mines. When they reach the coal, they use different machines to cut it from the rock. Long trains of carts carry the coal up to the surface. ◈ Oil and natural gas are reached by drilling into the earth. A big metal tower called a "Christmas tree" is then set up. It has pipes and special faucets called valves. Much like those in a kitchen faucet, the valves are used to turn the flow of oil on and off. They also adjust the speed at which the oil comes up the pipes. ◈ Many drills have tips made of diamonds, which can cut through even the hardest kinds of rock. Drills can cut through some rocks at up to 360 feet (110 m) per hour. Other rocks are so hard that the drill may move only a couple of inches (5 cm) per hour.

WORKERS DRILL FOR OIL
BOTH ON DRY LAND AND
UNDER THE OCEAN.

OIL AND OTHER FOSSIL
FUELS SUPPLY NEARLY
90 PERCENT OF THE
ENERGY USED IN THE
WORLD TODAY.

Oil is measured in barrels. One barrel

contains 42 gallons (159 l) of oil.

FOSSIL FUEL USES

ALL AROUND THE world, coal is used to make **electricity**. The coal is burned in stations called power plants, producing heat that is used to boil water. The steam from the hot water powers machines called generators, which produce electricity. Natural gas can be used in this way, too, but it is also burned to heat buildings and to run appliances such as clothes dryers and water heaters. Oil can also be used for heating, but it has many other uses. Oil that comes straight from the ground is called crude oil. People cannot do much with crude oil. However, once the oil has been treated at a refinery, it can be made into many different products. Oil is used to make **asphalt** for roads and fuel for cars, trucks, airplanes, and other machines. Grease for bicycle chains and other moving metal parts is made from oil. Carpets and clothing can be made from fibers that come from oil. Plastic products—including soda bottles and toys—come from oil. Even the soap we wash clothes and dishes with starts out as oil.

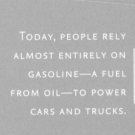

TODAY, PEOPLE RELY
ALMOST ENTIRELY ON
GASOLINE—A FUEL
FROM OIL—TO POWER
CARS AND TRUCKS.

A lot of gas and oil is found under the ocean floor. To retrieve it, large buildings and drills are built on floating platforms called oil rigs. The world uses more than 50 million barrels of oil per day. That's more than two billion gallons (7.6 billion l).

BECAUSE MOST OF THE
EARTH IS COVERED BY
WATER, A LOT OF OIL
CAN BE REACHED ONLY
FROM OIL RIGS.

THE FUTURE OF FOSSIL FUELS

PEOPLE USE FOSSIL fuels every day. They are good sources of energy that are cheap to find and use. They make our lives easier in many ways. But fossil fuels have some serious disadvantages, too. When they are burned, they produce smoke and dirt that **pollute** the air. This smoke goes up into the sky, where much of it is absorbed into the clouds. It then falls back to Earth as acid rain, which can hurt plants and animals. Another disadvantage is that there is a limited supply of these fuels. It took millions of years to make fossil fuels, and people are using them up quickly. Some experts think we may run out of them by the year 2060. Scientists are always trying to find other places on Earth where these fuels may be hidden. They are also searching for ways to reduce the smoke and dirt these fuels produce. They hope to find cleaner and safer ways to use these reliable sources of energy.

ONE OF THE MAIN DRAW-
BACKS TO USING FOSSIL
FUELS IS THE GREAT AMOUNT
OF POLLUTION THEY CAUSE.

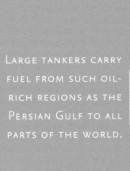

LARGE TANKERS CARRY
FUEL FROM SUCH OIL-
RICH REGIONS AS THE
PERSIAN GULF TO ALL
PARTS OF THE WORLD.

Huge ships called tankers carry oil across the ocean. They are so big that sometimes crew members use bicycles to get from one end to the other. Gas is used to make antifreeze, a liquid that keeps car engines from freezing up during the winter.

PEOPLE HAVE BEEN using fossil fuels for thousands of years. Oil that is black and sticky is called pitch. As far back as 2,000 years ago, it was painted on boats to make them waterproof. People also used pitch to make bright-burning torches. ◈ The Chinese have known about fossil fuels for centuries. During the 1200s, they were known to burn lumps of coal to keep warm. ◈ The first oil well was drilled on August 27, 1859, in Pennsylvania, when a man named Colonel Edwin Drake drilled 69 feet (21 m) into the earth and found oil. Soon, people all around the world started drilling into the ground to find this valuable fuel.

ALTHOUGH PEOPLE HAVE LONG KNOWN OF USES FOR OIL, COLLECTING IT WAS DIFFICULT UNTIL PUMPS WERE DEVELOPED.

⊙ Floating Oil   Oil weighs less than water. Often, when an oil well runs dry, water is pumped down the hole. Any oil left floats on top of the water, making it easy for workers to collect it. This experiment will prove that oil floats. You will need:

A bowl
Cooking oil
Water
Liquid dishwashing soap

⊙ Pour some cooking oil in the bowl. Then add a little bit of water. The oil will float on top of the water.

⊙ Sometimes, when oil is being carried by ships, accidents happen and oil is spilled. The oil floats on the water and may kill many animals nearby. To help clean up oil spills, workers use soaps.

⊙ Add a drop of dishwashing soap where the oil is pooling heaviest in the bowl. You'll see that the oil runs away from the soap.

Asphalt IS A COMBINATION OF OIL, GRAVEL, AND SAND THAT IS ROLLED OUT TO MAKE ROADS.

Electricity IS A TYPE OF ENERGY USED IN HOMES TO RUN LIGHTS AND APPLIANCES.

Gas fields ARE POCKETS IN THE EARTH WHERE NATURAL GAS IS FOUND.

To **pollute** THE AIR IS TO MAKE IT DIRTY.

Vapor IS A FORM OF GAS MADE OF VERY TINY DROPS OF LIQUID THAT HANG IN THE AIR.